IELTS WRITING TASK 2 SAMPLES

Over 50 High-Quality Model Essays for Your Reference to Gain a High Band Score 8.0+ In 1 Week (Book 12)

RACHEL MITCHELL

Copyright © 2017

All rights reserved.

ISBN: 9781973260196

TEXT COPYRIGHT © [RACHEL MITCHELL]

all rights reserved. No part of this guide may be reproduced in any form without permission in writing from the publisher except in the case of brief quotations embodied in critical articles or reviews.

Legal & disclaimer

The information contained in this book and its contents is not designed to replace or take the place of any form of medical or professional advice; and is not meant to replace the need for independent medical, financial, legal or other professional advice or services, as may be required. The content and information in this book have been provided for educational and entertainment purposes only.

The content and information contained in this book have been compiled from sources deemed reliable, and it is accurate to the best of the author's knowledge, information, and belief. However, the author cannot guarantee its accuracy and validity and cannot be held liable for any errors and/or omissions. Further, changes are periodically made to this book as and when needed. Where appropriate and/or necessary, you must consult a professional (including but not limited to your doctor, attorney, financial advisor or such other professional advisor) before using any of the suggested remedies, techniques, or information in this book.

Upon using the contents and information contained in this book, you agree to hold harmless the author from and against any damages, costs, and expenses, including any legal fees potentially resulting from the application of any of the information provided by this book. This disclaimer applies to any loss, damages or injury caused by the use and application, whether directly or indirectly, of any advice or information presented, whether for breach of contract, tort, negligence, personal injury, criminal intent, or under any other cause of action.

You agree to accept all risks of using the information presented inside this book.

You agree that by continuing to read this book, where appropriate and/or necessary, you shall consult a professional (including but not limited to your doctor, attorney, or financial advisor or such other advisor as needed) before using any of the suggested remedies, techniques, or information in this book.

TABLE OF CONTENT

SAMPLE 1 9

SAMPLE 2 11

SAMPLE 3 12

SAMPLE 4 14

SAMPLE 5 15

SAMPLE 6 16

SAMPLE 7 18

SAMPLE 8 20

SAMPLE 9 21

SAMPLE 10 23

SAMPLE 11 24

SAMPLE 12 27

SAMPLE 13 29

SAMPLE 14 30

SAMPLE 15 31

SAMPLE 16 33

SAMPLE 17 35

SAMPLE 18 36

SAMPLE 19 38

SAMPLE 20 39

SAMPLE 21 41

SAMPLE 22 42

SAMPLE 23 43

SAMPLE 24 44

SAMPLE 25 46

SAMPLE 26 48

SAMPLE 27 49

SAMPLE 28 51

SAMPLE 29 52

SAMPLE 30 53

SAMPLE 31 54

SAMPLE 32 55

SAMPLE 33 56

SAMPLE 34 57

SAMPLE 35 59

SAMPLE 36 60

SAMPLE 37 61

SAMPLE 38 63

SAMPLE 39 64

SAMPLE 40 65

SAMPLE 41 67

SAMPLE 42 68

SAMPLE 43 70

SAMPLE 44 71

SAMPLE 45 72

SAMPLE 46 73

SAMPLE 47 75

SAMPLE 48 77

SAMPLE 49 79

SAMPLE 50 80

SAMPLE 51 81

SAMPLE 52 82

CONCLUSION 84

CHECK OUT OTHER BOOKS 85

INTRODUCTION

Thank you and congratulate you for downloading the book *"IELTS Writing Task 2 Samples: Over 50 High-Quality Model Essays for Your Reference to Gain a High Band Score 8.0+ In 1 Week (Book 12)."*

This book is well designed and written by an experienced native teacher from the USA who has been teaching IELTS for over 10 years. She really is the expert in training IELTS for students at each level. In this book, she will provide you over 50 high-quality model essays to help you easily achieve an 8.0+ in the IELTS Writing Task 2, even if your English is not excellent. These samples will also walk you through step-by-step on how to develop your well-organized answers for the Task 2 Writing.

As the author of this book, I believe that this book will be an indispensable reference and trusted guide for you who may want to maximize your band score in IELTS task 2 writing. Once you read this book, I guarantee you that you will have learned an extraordinarily wide range of useful, and practical IELTS WRITING TASK 2 model essays that will help you become a successful IELTS taker as well as you will even become a successful English writer in work and in life within a short period of time only.

Take action today and start getting better scores tomorrow!

Thank you again for purchasing this book, and I hope you enjoy it.

SAMPLE 1

The crime rate in teenagers has increased dramatically in many countries in recent years. What are the causes, and what are the solutions?

In recent years, there has been a growing number of juvenile offences in many nations around the world. This is attributable to several reasons and can be addressed by some solutions.

To begin with, there are several causes that lead to the situation in which the crime rate among adolescents has climbed considerably. One of those causes is that parents in modern life usually hectic schedules, and may do not have enough time to take care of their children. Therefore, the children can do whatever they want and may have inappropriate behaviour such as participating in drug trafficking or stealing, which increases crime rates. Additionally, since teenagers nowadays have access to the Internet, juvenile crime becomes more organized, secure, and well-planned than it was in the past. For instance, most of the recruitment and crime planning work can be done constantly through a social network channel that vows to protect user's privacy, making it a challenge for the police to deter real crime in advance.

However, there are also a variety of solutions to alleviate this issue. The first solution is that parents need to pay more attention to their offspring. For example, by encouraging their children to take part in useful activities such as playing sports or studying music instruments, the children have a good chance to boost their cognitive development, which reduces crime rates. Moreover, Internet police can disguise themselves as normal young adults who wish to join those illegal groups for investigation and evidence gathering purposes. As a result, the police would have an opportunity to not only prevent the particular crime beforehand but also understand the underlying structure behind any contemporary juvenile crime.

In conclusion, there are some reasons why the crime rate in teenagers are increasing rapidly in today's world, and solutions should be produced to minimize the issue.

304 words

SAMPLE 2

Nowadays, young people admire sports stars though they often do not set a good example. Do you think this is a positive or negative development?

In recent years, the admiration young people hold for sports stars is not a new phenomenon. In spite of some scandals that may be occasionally displayed by a number of famous athletes, I strongly believe that the majority has a positive influence on young generations.

Firstly, sports celebrities are role models of reaching the top of career path through hardworking and self-discipline. No sportsman became successful without dedicating a part of their life to strict training and leading a healthy lifestyle. Therefore, youngsters will be inspired to participate in sports activities in an attempt to emulate their sports idols. Secondly, some well-known sportspeople have shown the extraordinary effort of overcoming adversity to achieve the success and this may motivate the youths to deal with such setbacks in their own lives. Neymar, for example, a football player, underwent a childhood in poverty in Brazil. But now, he is one of the most popular football stars, and his story has inspired many young people to strive for their own success.

Furthermore, sports stars play an important role in reminding youngsters about social responsibilities. Through their own charity activities, famous sportspeople can encourage their fans to contribute to the society. Cristiano Ronaldo is one of the most idolized football superstars in the world, but he still finds time to support charity events and inspire his fans to join charitable campaigns. At times, even a scandalous sportsman can surprisingly provide young people with moral lessons. A good image of this occurred when Canadian runner Ben Johnson lost his Olympic gold medal due to his illegal use of performance-enhancing drugs. This incident showed youngsters that drug use is a shameful behavior.

In conclusion, it seems to be clear that adolescents receive more benefits from sports stars through self-improvement and moral responsibilities.

297 words

SAMPLE 3

Some people believe that visitors to other countries should follow local customs and behavior. Others disagree and think that the host country should welcome cultural differences.

Discuss both these views and give your own opinion.

Give reasons for your answer and include any relevant examples from your own knowledge or experience.

In recent years, people tend to travel more frequently than ever before. While I agree that travelers should follow the host country's traditions and cultures, I also think that host country should welcome diversity of cultures.

On the one hand, there are various reasons why locals should accept and understand the different background of visitors. Firstly, it might be difficult for tourists to follow the customs and behaviors because of cultural differences, which are even incompatible with their belief and moral in some certain cases. Muslim people, for example, find it difficult to get used to Western foods. Secondly, native people have opportunities to learn good manners from foreigners, which might contribute to modern civilization. In particular, developing countries benefit enormously from this trend.

On the other hand, it will be beneficial for travelers if they adopt local cultures. The first benefit is that local people are more welcome when seeing foreigners show respects to indigenous customs. This establishment will definitely result in integration and mutual understand. Furthermore, it will be easier for visitors to blend into a new atmosphere, which enables them to engage with social activities of the host country such as festivals, national holidays and so on. The more events they participate in, the more life experience they gain. Finally, newcomers would probably avoid creating negative images if they conformed to the norm of social behaviors. The locals, for instance, will consider foreigners ill-mannered if they wear unsuitable clothes to go to church.

In conclusion, it seems to me that foreigners should adapt to local cultures because of benefits that they could gain and host country should also be opened to the cultural diversity of the newcomers.

280 words

SAMPLE 4

In many countries, people now wear Western clothes (suit, jeans) rather than traditional clothing.

Why? Is this a positive or negative development?

Nowadays, many citizens over the world give priority to Western clothes instead of traditional costumes. There are several reasons for this trend and in my opinion, this replacement brings out both benefits and drawbacks.

The reasons for the popularity of suits and jeans vary. Firstly, conventional customs are no longer appropriate and suitable for the modern life activities such as traveling or doing manual jobs. For example, Koreans rarely wear Hanbok on a daily basis due to its huge size which causes the inconvenience during walking. Furthermore, the expansion of Western-based corporations is another contributor to the preference for this so-called modern fashion style. Those organizations usually require their local staff to wear shirts and pants at work which gradually reshapes fashion patterns of the domestic citizens.

There are both advantages and disadvantages of this trend. On the one hand, when European clothing is available on the market, it gives people more choices of fashion to fulfill their requirements for fashion and beauty. Moreover, choosing Western clothes helps people integrate into the global working environment quickly, which is essential in the age of globalization. On the other hand, if such alternative becomes prevalent, the young generation might underestimate the meaning of traditional clothes which is considered old-fashioned items. In addition, no longer do people wear traditional customs, several local companies producing conventional customs would be put on the verge of bankruptcy. For instance, Vietnamese brocade clothing organizations are not active anymore due to the sharply declining traditional clothing consumption of the indigenous.

In conclusion, diverse factors could attribute to the widespread of European clothing and this phenomenon is positive and negative at the same time.

275 words

SAMPLE 5

When choosing a job, the salary is the most important consideration. To what extent do you agree or disagree?

Some people believe that salary plays a vital role in job decision. As far as I am concerned, candidates not merely attach their significance to their payroll but some other factors.

On the one hand, we should recognize that a reasonable salary level is very important when choosing a job. Firstly, a high salary is the facilitator of enhancing living standard. For instance, if people have more money, they can pay for their living expenses and all they want instead of for only what they truly need. Secondly, payment is the profound contribution to creating and encouraging people's working motivation which leads to efficient productivity and outstanding outcomes. Unless people have their own motivation, they may not work with 100% their energy and ability or overcome all obstacles and adversities. As a result, employers should recommend good wage because it is one of the most important considerations when a person chooses a work.

On the other hand, there are two other factors which are considered as extremely important criteria. First of all, the more satisfied on career, the longer a person works under their position. Job satisfaction is based on kind of work, payment for extra attempts, work environment and suitability to ideal job. Equally important, somebody chooses an occupation by its social value, which means the contribution that the work may make towards society because they might feel a sense of helpfulness to the community. Thus, a job, which ensures reasonable salary, job satisfactory and possessing its own benefits toward society, is the best of both worlds.

In conclusion, salary is very important but not a unique issue on job decision for a wide range of employees.

278 words

SAMPLE 6

Some teachers say students should be organized into groups to study, while others argue that students should be made to study alone.

Discuss both views and give your opinion?

There is an on-going disagreement among teachers on whether students should be arranged in groups to study or they should learn on their own. This essay will analyze both sides of the argument with sufficient proofs of my viewpoint.

On the one hand, studying alone offers several advantages to students. First, since students have to handle problems and answer questions by themselves when learning alone, they cannot rely on other people, which increases their independence. For example, learners individually can pace their learning and decide for themselves when to start and when to stop, enhancing the responsibility for their own learning process. Second, in order to concentrate well and make an efficient use of students' time, studying alone might allow learners to avoid being distracted by unnecessary interruptions and conversations with other people. For instance, I usually study in my university library which is very quiet, and I can learn faster and more effectively, which saves a tremendous amount of my time.

On the other hand, I believe group study exerts more positive aspects in some ways. To begin with, as each student has different abilities and knowledge, group members can encourage one another to improve their weaknesses. For example, when learning Math in a group, I can help my friends find out their mistakes. Therefore, my friends can avoid the same problems in the future, which positively affects their academic performances. In addition, since group members have to discuss and solve problems together, their communication skills and critical thinking abilities are greatly improved. In fact, because studying in a group requires students to interact constantly and share ideas, students have to listen to what their fellows say and debate with them if there is a disagreement.

In conclusion, while studying alone is beneficial to students to some extent, I believe studying in groups is a better option.

308 words

SAMPLE 7

Governments should spend money on railways rather than roads. To what extent do you agree or disagree with this statement?

MODEL ESSAY 1:

Finding ways to improve the transportation system is far from easy for governments. Some people think that governments should pour budget into the construction and development railway system rather than the improvement of current roads. I am in opposition to this idea and this essay tackles my most important reasons.

Firstly, proponents of favoring railways over others contend that the construction of railway is conducive to passengers thanks to its convenience. It might be true that by dint of railway systems along with the frequent and continuous operation of trains and subways, traveling from one province to another is easier. However, is it true under any circumstances? Facts have indicated that for the crowded cities where most of the residential areas and offices are located in narrow alleyways, traveling by trains becomes inconvenient and unfeasible. For example, for Hanoi City, which is famous for thirty-six old quarters and the intertwined streets, the dense appearance of the railways will make the transportation more complicated and as a result, locals will be, in most cases, bothered by its noise and uselessness instead of the appreciation for its convenience.

Secondly, supporters claim that the establishment of railways will save money for the government and citizens. It is likely that the existence of means of public transport such as the metro will help reduce the amount of fuel used by private vehicles. Nevertheless, does this option really save money? It is undeniable that along with the mass construction of railways is the mushrooming of stations, pick-up, and drop-off signs as well as security services, which costs a huge amount of public budget. Equally important, this policy also requires the re-organization and redesign of residential areas, universities, and hospitals to make way for the railway system. Behind this scenario lies a waste of money for hiring foreign experts and training engineers.

In conclusion, I strongly disagree with this policy for its waste of finance, inconvenience, and other potential dangers.

324 words

MODEL ESSAY 2:

Transportation system around the world has developed more widely and been better than it had been before. Some people claim that governments should invest more money in constructing railways instead of building roads. I strongly disagree with this statement because of its negative effects on the economy and environment of countries.

Firstly, it is believed that constructing railways is an effective solution for traffic congestion. Because of its large capacity, railways can transport a huge number of passengers at the same time. However, railway systems are only popular in large countries such as the USA, and Russia where terrains are beneficial to construct. Meanwhile, in regions where mountains and rivers are main landscapes, the investment of railways' construction takes up a huge amount of national budget, which jeopardizes the national economy. Besides, no sooner are railways erected than picturesque sceneries around these railways' areas are destroyed. Consequently, eco-tourism, which is considered to be a potential market of nations, is threatened.

In addition, although using trains is claimed to be beneficial to commuting a long distance, it is inconvenient to travel a short distance with flexible purposes. A scientific research has shown that people prefer cars or motorbikes to trains in their holidays. Besides, depending on natural and economic situations of each nation, to gain the highest efficiency, governments can apply different solutions such as raising people's awareness of participating in transporting or refurbishing the road systems.

In the final analysis, I am strongly against this solution for its backward impacts on the economy and environment of countries.

257 words

SAMPLE 8

Some people think that governments should ban dangerous sports, while others think people should have the freedom to do any sports or activities. Discuss both views and give your opinion.

Recently, there has been a tendency to take up sports which involve risky activities as a hobby, especially among young people. Some people believe that these kinds of sports should be banned by the governments, while others argue that it is their own right to take part in any leisure activities. Although I side with the latter opinion, this essay will examine both perspectives.

On the one hand, the act of the government prohibiting dangerous sports is understandable, because if unexpected accidents happen, the consequence will be a burden on families and, in a way, impact the society. First, at the scale of family, in case fatal accidents occur to a member, the rest of the family will not only be affected emotionally but also monetarily due to the loss of a financial support. Moreover, it is likely that those who participate in such risky activities will foster an irresponsible lifestyle. At a larger scale, such lifestyle may impose a negative influence on younger generations, thereby affecting the society to some extent.

On the other hand, I believe some people take up risky sports for certain benefits. First of all, it brings about the release of stress from the tedium of daily life. Nowadays, there is evidence that people always immerse themselves with the repetition of work inside concrete buildings. Therefore, the unprecedented experience from doing skydiving or bungee jumping helps them to get away from the hustle and bustle of life. Furthermore, to several people, those activities offer the chance to discover a new way of life, leading, more or less, to innovation which is necessary for jobs which require creativity. In this sense, it paves the way for work efficiency.

In conclusion, even though there are some reasons for the governments to forbid risk-taking sports, it is up to each individual's freedom to decide which activities are suitable for them.

312 words

SAMPLE 9

Nowadays environmental problems are too big to be managed by individual persons or individual countries. In other words, it is an international problem. To what extent do you agree or disagree?

Pollution issues these days are too serious to be solved by only a group of people or countries. Moreover, pollution is considered a huge global problem. In my opinion, I believe that environmental contamination is the top priority of the entire world.

To begin with, one of the reasons why the environment is regarded as an international problem is that it can be easily observed from numerous articles, television news and daily newspaper due to its appearance in every country. All the social media have recently reported on the terrible cause of pollutants as well as low air and water quality in a large number of developing countries. For instance, in China, smog is the most major concern which puts the country at risk of warming, greenhouse effect and rapid decrease in residents' living condition. Although measures are being taken by the government at the present time, fumes and gas emission from factories and power stations cannot completely vanish. Furthermore, China is not the only country facing bad environmental quality, other countries such as Viet Nam, India, and Thailand are also dealing with plenty of issues like industrial waste, deposited rubbish, carbon dioxide and so on. Apparently, the widespread contamination is devastating almost every place in the world.

Secondly, it is undeniable that environmental pollution's negative impact on the earth is substantial. A great quantity of waste released from factories is likely to destroy the ecosystem especially the marine life. Besides, it also poisons the nearby river, lake, stream, and ocean. In the same way, poisonous air and source of water can have a detrimental impact on inhabitants' well-being. For example, sickness, headache, exhaustion are becoming increasingly prevalent among global citizens since they are suffering from a change in climate, global warming along with polluted and unsafe food. In addition, scientists believe that contaminated heath can lead to abnormal following generations, which is extremely dangerous.

In summary, nowadays contamination is the largest worldwide concern due to its high level of considerable damage to all of the nations in the world.

330 words

SAMPLE 10

People should follow the customs and traditions when people start to live in a new country.

To what extent do you agree or disagree?

Many people believe that foreigners should adapt to local customs and traditions when they come to settle down in another country. I completely agree with this point of view.

Immigrants will definitely encounter a number of difficulties if they do not adopt the norms of social behavior in the new country. Firstly, it would be almost impossible for them to integrate into a new living environment. For example, it will be wiser if an entrepreneur, who resides in another nation and opens his new own business, obeys market law and regulations of the host country. Secondly, law violation is likely an inevitable consequence. In Singapore, for example, newcomers certainly will be considered as dirty and ill-mannered if they litter in the ground or split chewing gum in public places.

There are many advantages for foreigners stemming from following the customs and traditions. The very first benefit is that local citizens will become more hospitable when respect for cultural practices from newcomers can be seen. As a result, forging strong bonds with native people will be simpler, enabling a greater integration and mutual understanding. The second advantage is the richness of precious experiences which foreigners can accumulate by engaging themselves in a range of ethnic festivals and cultural holidays. Thus, social isolation can be avoided naturally and a sense of community in new nation gradually is formed, which are profound conditions to stabilize and start a new life.

In conclusion, I would contend that following the customs and traditions of the adopted country should be seriously taken by foreigners who want to blend into new society and build a new life in another country as well.

275 words

SAMPLE 11

The continued rise in the world's population is the greatest problem faced by humanity at the present time.

What are the causes of this continued rise?

Do you agree that it is the greatest problem faced by humanity?

Give reasons for your answer and include any relevant examples from your own knowledge or experience.

<u>**MODEL ESSAY 1:**</u>

We are living in a world of globalization where knowledge is exchanged across nations and continents. In many universities around the world, there are a certain proportion of international students. This development, however, presents both its positive and negative effects in specific cases.

On the one hand, international students may find studying abroad bring them with a great many opportunities for their career. The first incentive can be the international qualifications. It is obvious that qualifications of this type are exclusively provided by countries with the best education systems. For example, the USA, the UK or Australia are the top 3 countries that people choose to take undergraduate or post-graduate courses because of the international prestigious education they provide. With qualifications from these addresses, many believe paths to better jobs and successful career will be wide opened for them. Besides, relations are also what foreign students will possibly be entitled from international studying environment. This stands as a great opportunity for them to form a future professional network, which is a key to a successful career in the future.

On the other hand, the most common stake students may encounter is a culture shock. People suffering from this drawback will find themselves difficult to fit in and gradually become stressed and discouraged in studying. Moreover, from a macroscopic perspective, abroad education may negatively impact the growth of the both sending and receiving countries. People that have jobs in the country where they study often find a way to settle down and not come back, which may contribute a significant loss of labour force to their home country. In return, countries receiving international students may have to take care of more citizens, which may be a burden to the government budget and a risk to the stability of our society.

To sum up, parallel with the globalization process, the gap between developing and developed countries are being narrowed. The quality of education in some developing countries has greatly improved. Therefore, although abroad education brings about many benefits people tend to study at home to avoid above-mentioned possible risks.

330 words

MODEL ESSAY 2:

Overpopulation is one of the greatest fears of mankind not because of its terrifying consequences but also bad impacts on humanity. Scientists around the world are trying to figure out the roots of the continued rise population in order to reduce the risks of overpopulation.

The population is contributed by each member of our society; therefore, individuals and their activities are the first to blame for the ever-rising population. Parents who are unaware of the risks of overpopulation tend to give birth to many children. In particular, developing countries such as India, China or countries in Africa, there is even a concept among a majority of citizens that family with many members will have wealth and prosperity; therefore, each year a significant number of newborns are being added to the population. Besides, governments are also responsible for the expansion of the demography. No rules enacted to regulate the number of children born in each family contributes to worsening the problem. The situation witnessed in China under the ruling of President Mao who desired for a great China and encourages multiple reproductions among Chinese families showed that a tremendous population could lead to detrimental effects one of which was the Great Famine in China in the early 50s.

The consequences of a rising population are countless and unable to reverse. Many social outcomes can be crimes, poverty or even famine. Population interconnected with many aspects of the society, therefore, the by-products of overpopulation could harm the world's economy and even security. To solve the problem is a complex task of humanity as it is impossible to reduce the number of the population, yet ease the consequences when the population is still so large.

To sum up, facing such a problem individuals and governments should join hand to improve the situation. Proper regulations should be imposed in order to reduce the rising rate of the population and people have to be aware of the alarming affair to take right actions.

328 words

SAMPLE 12

Some people get into debt by buying things they don't need and can't afford.

What are the reasons for this behaviour?

What action can be taken to prevent people from having this problem?

We are living in a society where goods and services are becoming so abundant that choosing the right things to buy sometimes confuses consumers. Some people end up being indebted for spending on unnecessary goods and services or expensive things for which they are unable to pay. This tendency, which is driven by several reasons, should be halted by serious actions from individuals and governments.

In the modern world today, access to goods and services is made so easy and convenient that many people have become shopaholics. Inventions created to assist shopping such as credit card or online stores make people have quicker and less cautious shopping decisions. In addition, this tendency can be mostly witnessed in some teenagers and groups of young people who buy things which are luxurious and expensive because they want to show others they have style and to save face in front of their friends. To elaborate, these components of the society tend to spend on trends so that they can feel fit in among their peers. However, the dangerous thing is that most of them do not have a career with stable income and are not immature enough to make proper decisions; therefore, they fall into debt easily buying inessentials just to paint their ego.

To stop these behaviours, there are several possible solutions. Firstly, the financial system should have stricter regulations to reduce the number of unreliable transactions. For example, credit cards should only be provided to people who can prove they are able to afford using beforehand payment and have the stable salary to pay back credit card expense monthly to the bank. Besides, families are also responsible to teach their kids how to spend money properly and respect the value of money in order for them not to make incautious shopping decisions when they become mature.

To sum up, spending money properly has always been a difficult task;

however, governments and families should take actions such as stricter control in the financial system or early teaching children how to use money to prevent people from falling into debt for spending too much on inessentials.

328 words

SAMPLE 13

Some people say that history can teach us many important values and lessons, but others think it is unnecessary to learn from the past. Discuss both views and give your own opinion.

It is argued that whether the role of historical knowledge in society is essential or not. While there are benefits from history, there are also favorable reasons why former things are dispensable.

On the one hand, historical understanding brings numerous meaningful stories and traditional concepts. Firstly, civilian can recognize the origin of their race thousand years ago. Moreover, they can also discover the establishment and existence of the state in which they are living at the beginning until present. Additionally, long-ago lectures consist of fearless heroes or sacrificial individuals who contributed so much to the country's independent protection. Secondly, thanks to history, each person will be enhanced the awareness of such proud periods and therefore extend their national pride. Through such important values, everyone can strengthen consciousness of protection for our nation as well as the worldwide peace.

On the other hand, studying what happened in the past is just waste of time. Firstly, those facts, names or time are abundant information to be memorized by people's brain as they cannot be put into in practical or daily life of everyone. Secondly, people should spend time on others required fields for further demands. It should be made emphasis on technology or science aspects for application into reality to reach a better life in a modern environment.

In conclusion, it seems evident that the opinion of learning history as a principal subject and the idea of considering it as a minor factor have their own unique advantages. However, I firmly believe that teacher should introduce more skills to get a better job in the future rather than mainly focus on demonstrating ancient events.

272 words

SAMPLE 14

Movies are popular all over the world. Explain why movies are popular.

There is no doubt that movies are prevalent for all ages and genders all over the world. The technological advancement, highly entertaining abilities and conveyance of incisive meanings are three reasons why films are increasingly widespread across all kinds of people.

To begin with, one of the most obvious reasons why movies are popular is the outstanding development of technologies. For example, viewers can instantaneously reserve movie tickets or watch movies via the Internet on their computers and smartphones instead of arriving at the cinemas. In addition, incredibly special effects designed by brilliant software and applications strengthen fascination and attraction in films. Advanced technology equipment not only creates a spectacular appearance for movies, but also it provides the public with a straightforward access to films.

Another reason for the popularity of moves is that films entertain viewers so that they can achieve happiness. Watching films is a way to reduce tension after audiences coping with mishaps and difficulties in daily lives. With an upsurge in workload, it is thoroughly a good idea to escape from extreme pressure by enjoying movies.

Furthermore, films have the capability to connect people together because they convey insightful messages to audiences. For instance, emotional films bearing love meanings foster, enhance and associate family relationship. As a consequence of an increase in production of meaningful movies, there are a growing number of viewers craving for applying significant messages in films into reality.

In conclusion, there are various reasons why movies become popular all over the world. Thanks to technological breakthroughs, amusing abilities, and great significances, this period is certain to be the prosperous era of the film industry.

272 words

SAMPLE 15

Some parents buy their children a large number of toys to play with. What are the advantages and disadvantages for the child of having a large number of toys?

Give reasons for your answer and include any relevant examples from your own knowledge or experience.

It is true that many young people nowadays receive a multitude of playthings from their parents. This essay will firstly, discuss children's distraction as one of the main disadvantages of this trend, and secondly, outline increasing creativity as one of the main advantages.

To begin with, there are some downsides when parents purchase various toys for their offspring. Firstly, owning multiple playthings could be detrimental to youngsters. To be more specific, the concentration of the children will probably be suffered if there are too many tempting objects which constantly surround them. The children will eventually get more and more distracted. Secondly, a large majority of toys are made of plastic, which commonly contains the chemical compound. This could result in negatively affected health, especially when young people suck or touch them frequently. Finally, on the social side, those who possess far more playthings than their classmates might be a target of envy. As a result, their relationship could be unstable.

However, I strongly believe that the benefits are more significant than such disadvantages. A reason for this is that toys obviously stimulate the creativity of each child. My son, for example, can create dinosaurs –shaped or rocket – shaped thing from small plastic bricks. Another reason is that many modern playthings are designed to aim at the early educational purpose for children. It is definitely easier for children to learn the number and alphabet with board toys which are equipped with sounds. Consequently, toys are useful for education as long as parents carefully choose the right products.

In conclusion, it seems to me that the advantages of this tendency such as developing the creativity in each child outweigh the drawbacks namely distraction.

281 words

SAMPLE 16

Discuss the advantages and this advantages of studying abroad.

Nowadays, studying overseas is gaining more and more popularity with students, undergraduates or postgraduates entire the world. While some people are of the opinion that the pattern of this learning can bring various merits to those, opponents of the idea claim that the shortcomings eclipse the benefits.

On the one hand, there are a variety reasons exist and explain why people choose to study abroad instead of learning in their own countries. The first considerable explanation is that students will have a chance to be trained in the contemporary and academic environment. For instance, if we study at schools, colleges or universities in many developed countries namely: Harvard, Stanford, Princeton, we will be given lectures by well-known and well-qualified professors. Moreover, we can approach a large number of new learning methods such as integrated methods instead of state education in many developing nations. The final reason is that the degree or certificate and in-depth knowledge about our major which we receive and acquire from these universities can enhance our employment opportunities. For example, many students choose to study in Japan because Japan has numerous multinational companies with a high salary, but Japan has a minority of the workforce.

On the other hand, there have a variety negative aspects of studying overseas. Firstly, we will face to financial burden because the cost of living in abroad and tuition is expensive. Parents have to use all their financial resources to pay for fees and if they cannot have enough money, those children have to work many part-time jobs to earn money for subsistence fee or course's fee. It can lead them to neglect their studies and just concentrate on how to make money. Secondly, cultural handles and language barriers are huge issues which student abroad have to face. Furthermore, they can feel lonely and sad when they stay apart from their parents.

In conclusion, we should choose a school which is suitable for our conditions and finance and had better consider about the limitations of studying abroad.

330 words

SAMPLE 17

Some people think that it is best to live in a vertical city (mean that people work and live in high buildings) while others think a horizontal city is better. Discuss both views and give your opinion.

In recent years, an increasing number of people choose to live in a vertical city. Many people believe that it is the best way, whereas others believe that living in a horizontal city is more comfortable. In my opinion, I think the first viewpoint prefers to the model life now.

On the one hand, it is undeniable that ground-based area has many benefits. Firstly, people have to pay less for building services. It seems evident that living in a detached accommodation will save a great deal of spending on elevator, sanitation or parking fee. These such feats hold a part of monthly expenditure, instead of this, people will have money for making the most out of annual vacation. Secondly, living lower to the ground is safer for inhabitant what emergencies occur. In fact, there are many accidents such as fire, short-circuit happened in some apartments and many victims cannot go out because they dwell on high floor.

However, living in a vertical area, in my opinion, have more facilities than the area mentioned above. Firstly, residents can enjoy many attached services like gym fitness, swimming pool, and shopping mall right in their own apartment block. This enables people to have an integral life easily. Secondly, with the vertical city, the public infrastructure will be modern and suitable. The government will have more space to build some public use such as hospitals, schools or green parks. Besides, in urban areas, the overpopulation is more concerned, thus living in a department is one of the solutions to less pressure for housing facilities.

In conclusion, it is debatable whether living in the vertical or horizontal area. However, I believe that apartment building is more suitable modernization process now.

285 words

SAMPLE 18

It is observed that in many countries not enough students are choosing study science subject.

What are causes? And what will be effects on society?

There is no doubt that the lack of science students is a pressing matter in several nations. The reasons for this are varied; and without state intervention, this situation will take tolls on the development of human society.

The low awareness of the importance of science amongst disadvantaged people and the poor quality of education in developing countries are the two main factors contributing to the limited number of science learners. First and foremost, suffering from financial burdens, poverty-stricken families hardly have opportunities to expose to modern devices as well as an understanding of how the enhancement of science and technology will change people's lives. As a result, these parents tend to send their children to vocational schools rather than science educators so as to land manual jobs. Furthermore, the absence of excellent science professors and scientific research facilities in most of Third World countries makes their colleges fail to educate qualified graduates and guarantee students' career prospects.

This phenomenon will predispose the backward economy and society in the future. To commence with, as science knowledge is applied in almost every key factors of an economy from health care to manufacture, the scarcity of professionals such as doctors or scientists and valuable research results in these fields has a tendency to make the production and service sectors come to a halt and fall behind as compared to those in wealthy countries. To be equally important, due to the absence of knowledge of science in life, a society seems to be uncivilized and inconvenient. To illustrate, in rural parts of impoverished nations, not only do old-fashioned production methods induce environmental pollution but depraved customs also fuel societal unrest.

In conclusion, there are two main causes of few students pursuing science disciplines in many countries. As a consequence, their economy and society will bear the brunt of this trend in the future.

309 words

SAMPLE 19

Some people say that it is possible for a country to be both economically successful and have a clean environment. Others disagree. Discuss both views and give your opinion.

There has been an opinion that a country can possess a successful economy and a 'green' environment at the same time, while some people disagree with this point of view, saying that one cannot be achieved without the expense of the other. Although personally, I am in favour of the former statement, this essay will examine both perspectives.

On the one hand, admittedly, it is likely that a nation can be successful in terms of economy at the expense of a sound environment. This case is especially true for countries whose prosperity is dependent on natural resources. Over-reliance on economic growth, they capitalize on every available resource of nature, thereby putting such resources on the verge of exhaustion and causing ecological imbalance. A standard example for this is China, an industrialized country with the most rapid growth rate. As a result of overexploitation of nature, this nation is now facing a high level of pollution and risk of environmental degradation, according to a recent report in related field.

On the other hand, there is evidence of countries achieving both targets at the same time. It can be easily seen in economies emphasizing on the knowledge-based industry, which attracts a great number of white-collar workers with specialized skills. Take Singapore for instance. It acquires a reputation for a well-developed economy while still maintaining a harmonized environment. Moreover, its citizens have a high awareness of environmental conservation. It should also be noted that recently, many developed countries have put a considerable amount of their national budget on the research of environmentally friendly manufacturing methods to suppress the consequences of damaging the ecosystem.

In conclusion, it is feasible for a country to obtain an economic success and a clean environment simultaneously.

288 words

SAMPLE 20

Some people think that certain prisoners should be made to do unpaid community work instead of being put behind bars. To what extent do you agree or disagree?

Many people hold the belief that forcing criminals to serve community service is more beneficial than imprisonment. In my point of view, I believe that doing community work is the most appropriate punishment for offenders in certain cases/ I totally agree with this idea.

To begin with, non-paying jobs should be entitled to people especially minors who commit an insignificant crime. Such jobs act as a more effective deterrent than prison since the criminals just need a short interval of time to improve their behavior that the lengthy prison sentence is not suitable. For example, when offenders are convicted to steal modest objects like/ such as a watch, a bag, small quantity of money and so on, the jury can tackle the case by forcing them to do community services for hours. Besides, the individuals who just steal few things often have acceptable manner and their guilty action is usually temporary. Therefore, works which benefit the society should be handled by them. Apparently, unpaid work is the best option to solve minor cases so that the society is enhanced and the criminals are justifiably punished at the same time.

Secondly, another advantage of prisoners doing community service is that it prevents over-crowed offenders in local prison. Since the crime is increasing dramatically in the present time, more and more guilty people are put in prison. In that case, a court of law will choose to sentence the criminals by giving them non-paying jobs instead of incarceration. Moreover, this measure taken by the jury can also reduce lack of supervision in prison as well as avoid locating minor criminals in and harsh and detrimental prison environment. Thanks to such advantages, it is undeniable that the community work policy for the minor prisoners works very effectively.

In summary, community services are considered as the more proper way to punish slightly guilty prisoners rather than imprison them in some particular cases.

318 words

SAMPLE 21

Many parents go to work in other countries, taking their families with them, do you think the advantages overweigh the disadvantages.

Nowadays, many working parents accompany their family members overseas to work. Personally, I think this trend has both benefits and drawbacks for/ owning to the following reasons.

On the one hand, expatriates may encounter some difficulties when leaving the home country. Indeed, all members will face a lot tremendous problems to integrate with the new environment. For example, not only parents but their children have to learn the new foreign language to eliminate language/ communication barrier as well. Besides, all people have to spend a lot of time discovering tradition and custom of different countries to actually become real citizens. Equally important, if parents cannot have a stabilize incomes, it is difficult to meet their basic needs such as foods, clothes, water fees as well as children's tuition fees.

On the other hand, leaving their home to work with family members actually creates some precious opportunities for both parents and children. If the new nation destination is the developed areas, parents have the ability to continue pursuing their dreams and earning more money to support their relatives. Furthermore, children certainly have a chance to approach advanced education and good medical healthcare systems. Therefore, the next generation will certainly get a great deal of real experience, obtain valuable knowledge and have a healthy body in the future.

In conclusion, I hold my view that taking their family when going to work in other nations has advantages as well as disadvantages.

255 words

SAMPLE 22

As the number of car increases, more money has to be spent on road systems. Some people believe think the government should pay for this. Others think that the drivers should cover the costs. Discuss both views and give your opinion.

As a result of city sprawling and the fast pace of life, there is a growing body of evidence that the number of private cars is on the rise. And this has sparked a controversy about whether the costs of improving road facilities should be covered by the government or car owners. In my opinion, both parties should jointly shoulder the financial burden. This essay will discuss both perspectives.

On the one hand, the government certainly holds responsibility for upgrading infrastructure facilities of road systems. One justification is that the government can accumulate a national budget from taxes, which are derived from citizens' personal incomes and other sources. Similarly important to note is that the road systems are of public utility, and the government's actions are based on the well-being of the people. Therefore, the national authority should represent all citizens, contributing to cover the costs/expense improving the systems. Ok, clear main points, clear reason, coherent

On the other hand, drivers should also incur a part of the costs, because the increase in car ownership has led to a number of serious issues ranging from traffic congestion, road degradation to air pollution. It should be noted that some developed countries have already posted those costs on drivers in the form of road fees charging for cars entering city centres. In this sense, the national authority is likely to raise more funds for the road upgradation.

In conclusion, it is reasonable that both the government and owners of private cars ought to be mutually responsible for the amount of money dedicated to the investment in the road systems.

267 words

SAMPLE 23

The animal species are becoming extinct due to human activities on land and in the sea.

What are the reasons and solutions?

Over the past few decades, industrialization and modernization have been fostered in leaps and bounds. Going hand in hand with economic development is the environmental deterioration, resulting in the disappearance of animal species. In the following essay, the main culprit of this phenomenon, human activities, and settlements will be analyzed.

Wittingly or unwittingly, aquatic and terrestrial habitats have been polluted significantly due to mankind's daily routine in recent years. Indeed, deforestation to pave the way for new factories and overpopulation undermines creatures' melting pot, killing an array of wild animals. For instance, in Asia countries, more and more animals are standing at on the verge of extinction due to logging. In terms of water environment, not to mention poisons from domestic wastes, cultural festivals of some nations should be responsible for the diminishing diversification of natural species. In Denmark, the growth of young men is honored by thousands of whale lives every year, coloring its sea red.

To tackle this status, proactive actions must be taken by both individuals and governments. Authorities should enact stricter laws to preserve forest areas, which is a good stepping-stone for protecting wild animals. When it comes to religious norms, governments have to raise public's awareness about animal's right and launch other eco-friendly campaigns for their citizens to attend, instead of current brutal rules.

In conclusion, humans must be accountable for what they have done to animal species. From my perspective, social progress and old-fashioned mindset are the root causes of this problem. Only by pooling both personal and national efforts can we save the endangered creatures.

262 words

SAMPLE 24

Some people think the best way to solve global environmental problem is to increase the cost of fuel. To what extent do you agree or disagree?

Raising the price of fossil fuels is considered as the most effective way to deal with environmental warming. The question of whether raising fossil fuel price could resolve environmental issues remains a source of controversy. While I believe that this may suit many people, I would argue that there are a large number of substitutes which can be imposed to preserve the environment apart from increasing cost.

On the one hand, there are a variety of reasons why boosted fuel expenditure is a reliable method to reduce global warming. Firstly, fossil fuels such as coal, petrol, and oil with high cost easily turn down the customers, therefore, fuels consumption will dwindle sharply and fewer pollutants from burning fossil fuels process are released. In fact, the scientists prove that the carbon dioxide from the fuel combustion devastates the ozone layer, which leads to greenhouse effect along with numerous problems. However, this issue can be tackled as residents refuse to use petrol, gasoline, and oil since such fuels cost a great deal. Secondly, expensive fuels cause companies which are specialized in exploiting natural resources to be restrained; as a result, the environment will not be destroyed any further. In addition, when the price of fuels grows up, the purchase will occur more difficulty and the exploitation will be restricted, therefore, the environmental destruction by humans will be stopped immediately.

On the other hand, other feasible measures should also be taken into consideration in an effort of protecting the environment. For example, alternative energy is one of the best choices to replace fossil fuels. It is renewable and infinite thanks to the innovation of sophisticated technology and the Mother Nature. By using some panels located on the roof of the house, the sun rays are readily trapped and transformed into electricity to meet the basic need of the local inhabitants. Besides, the transformation is very environmentally friendly since it has no detrimental impact on the surrounding atmosphere. Another method to achieve the success in bettering environment is population reducing. Nowadays, the over-populated concern can link to the tremendous household waste as well as carry more potential environmental risks. Furthermore, the huge waste deposited in the ocean contaminates sharply the marine life. Moreover, when this rubbish decomposes, more and more poisonous gas is given off and it is also a contributor to low air quality and global warming. Apparently, lessening the trend in population means limitation in the aforementioned pollution.

To summary, the high fuels cost policy plays an important role in keeping the environment fresh. Nevertheless, other strategies like alternative energy and population reduction are also vital for the environmental revolution.

330 words

SAMPLE 25

Nowadays, universities and colleges are recruiting more and more students.

What do you think about this idea?

There are increasing number students who enroll in universities after entrance examination and evaluation to become university students. I completely agree with this idea that universities and colleges should acquire many new students.

There are numerous reasons why students should be presented an equal position in institutions or colleges. One reason is that universities are creating substantial opportunities for many students to achieve important knowledge, helpful experience, and be mature in their lives to pursue their dream. For instance, if a student studied at university, he could do his best to earn valuable degree such as DC agree or Bachelor's degree and if another attended in vocational school, he perhaps would lose his motivation to make his dream come true. Furthermore, more and more students attending in universities and colleges will evolve civilization. The civilization increase means that the standard of living, the education and behavior will be totally enhanced. In fact, the more a man learns and undergoes, the more abilities he will contribute to society.

Apart from the practical explanations expressed above, I believe that an examination cannot exactly evaluate almost the ability of attendees trying to attend in universities and colleges. A test may be appropriate for one, but not for others. Besides, the result is also based on the luckiness of participants. Therefore, this idea mentioned above is extremely progressive. For example, in the United States, the process of education like a funnel, which means that it is not difficult to study at university but you must work efficiently to a significant degree. Instead of focusing on the number, America tries to improve their quality of education.

In conclusion, I believe that recruiting a great number of students studying universities and colleges should be widely spread in all countries over the world.

296 words

SAMPLE 26

Some people say that parents should control their children's behavior from a very young age. What do you think?

Many people hold the belief that children at the early stage must be under strict supervision of their parents. While I accept that this may sound logical and suitable many cases, I believe that giving freedom to children to the certain extent would give them more chances to improve their own.

On the one hand, there are a variety of reasons why people should control their children at young age. One reason is that the very first place for the babies to learn is their own home and their first teacher is their parents. If both mother and father give the children good etiquette such as doing practices to make them behave properly and understand the rules as well as traditions in home, they will treat people in good social manner. It is also beneficial for them in their upcoming life. Furthermore, being given right direction from their parents will help children to understand the difference between right and wrong, also their rights and responsibilities in the community. Consequently, children are more capable of following the proper direction to achieve goals in their lives and contributing to developing a better society all around.

On the other hand, reasonable control from parents enables children to develop in an appropriate way. They are predicted to be more able to make decisions regarding various aspects of life in future. For example, letting children be free to learn under the provision of parents would make their imagination and living skills much better. In that way, they can grow up with the style of thinking outside the box which makes them find more interesting ideas or goals to achieve in their life.

In conclusion, it is certainly true that being under parents' control is an important factor for the growing-up of children, but this will work better for them if parents can make a good balance between controlling and letting their children free.

318 words

SAMPLE 27

Increasingly, the western world has been outsourcing its labor-related jobs to cheaper alternatives available in less-developed countries. Although this creates opportunities for people in poorer nations, it is a policy that is criticized by many in the west.

Write an essay response supporting the case for outsourcing of labour related jobs.

Give reasons for your answer and include any relevant example from your knowledge or experience.

The issue of outsourcing labor has been becoming a heated controversy. While this tendency has some clear advantages, it also has several drawbacks.

On the one hand, the benefits of outsourcing companies and workers vary. Firstly, these companies find low labor cost enticing. This not only helps them cut down a huge amount of costs but also confront a looming shortage of skillful employees and the state of raising salary facing them in the home country. For example, Western European corporations tend to outsource largely to India, where a vast of well-trained people are willing to work for a lower payment than residents in their nations. Secondly, workers subcontracting work to another company have more job opportunities with well-paid jobs and good job prospects, compared to the per capita income in their own country. This source of income effectively contributes to the enhancement/ improvement of their living standard.

On the other hand, the shortcomings of this trend are also undeniable. First, a preponderance of outsourcing organizations tends to neglect their own workforce in the home country. Because a source of cheaper white-collar workers and more skilled blue-collar workers are available in developing countries such as China or Philippines. Thus, residents of these countries may become unemployed and a degradation of the quality of life. Another positively related result may be the residents' unemployment index that ruins the economy as well as other social issues such as crime rate, revenue tax.

In conclusion, while outsourcing organizations and outsourcing workers derive benefits from this shift, this trend may cause several negative effects on corporations' home country.

265 words

SAMPLE 28

Children in many countries are eating more fast food and convenience snacks.

Why are children doing this and how serious are the consequences?

Give reasons for your answer and include any relevant examples from your own knowledge or experience.

Junk food is gaining more and more popularity among people, especially the young over the world. This essay will first discuss several reasons for this trend and then address the question of how serious the result for children is.

The reasons for the prevalence of fast food vary. Initially, it is undeniable that fast food brings convenience to customers. Rather than eating a meal in a restaurant, it only takes a couple minutes to buy fast food and take away. In addition, fast food shops are being opened every day at every corner of the street and these shops are approachable and reasonably priced. Furthermore, there is an excessive number of advertisements for junk foods namely hamburgers or pizza in the media, which are making the efforts to persuade young people to follow this diet trend. It, therefore, will affect the children's choices of foods to some extent.

However, this tendency brings some significant downsides to youngsters. Firstly, health-related problems associated with fast food are at an alarming rate. It is scientifically proven that daily consumption of fast food will lead to obesity in the long term. Secondly, funk foods do not provide enough nutrients for children which may detrimentally affect children's development. At this stage of life, children need many kinds of vitamin/protein and minerals to support their body. The lack of them can affect physical and mental development in each child.

In conclusion, there are a number of reasons why many children are likely to opt for fast foods on a regular basis and several disadvantages have been raised to be aware people of this trend.

269 words

SAMPLE 29

People in the community can buy cheaper products nowadays. Do the advantages outweigh the disadvantages?

Nowadays, consumers are able to purchase more affordable products. While I accept its significant benefits, I am of the opinion that the drawbacks outweigh them.

On the one hand, there are a variety of reasons why buying cheaper good is beneficial. The foremost merit of these is that more people can afford a wider range of goods and services with lower costs, especially people who usually struggle with financial situations. In other words, consumers nowadays are able to have a better standard of living with high-tech devices such as smart TVs and smartphones without spending much of their tight budget which help them save a lot of money for other vital expenses. Furthermore, cheaper products undoubtedly stimulate/ encourage people to consume more. Therefore, the national economy will be boosted as a result of raising productivity in order to meet the increasing demand. There will be more jobs created, reducing the unemployment rate; therefore, this will benefit the whole society.

On the other hand, the shortcomings of this trend cannot be ignored. Firstly, cheap products are usually associated with poor quality due to the face that manufacturers tend to use low-quality materials and low-skilled workers in order to reduce the production costs. Consumers may feel disappointed because the items they bought are not as durable as the expected. For example, products produced in China are complained about its low quality, despite the competitive prices of such products. Secondly, there are several harmful impacts on the environment caused by the use of unsafe materials. This is most notably in agriculture, where farmers use unlabeled cheap pesticides to increase productivity, which pollutes soil water sources.

In conclusion, besides the merits which can be pointed out from cheap products, I am strongly convinced that the disadvantages of low-priced products overshadow its advantages.

298 words

SAMPLE 30

It is impossible to help all people in the world, so government should only focus on people in their own countries. Do you think this is a positive or negative development?

In the shifting 21st century, the world is on the way of improvement with the aid of staggering technology advancements; these enhance people's living conditions getting wealthier than ever before. Therefore, giving a hand to support the other countries which are poorer does not seem to be an impossible mission.

On the one hand, it is true that many people are still living in the poverty and cannot support themselves. They are struggling with an empty stomach, maybe, for the rest of their life; living in shabby conditions. Thus, the government of countries with prosperous economy should introduce some viable/ feasible solutions to help the under developing countries pass over these difficult stages. Simultaneously, giving a call to citizens to let them have an awareness of sympathy and contribute a little thing such as food, clothes and other necessities into the charities will help these people a lot to recover quickly. By this way, the image of this country will be enhanced and well-known by international peers leading to various advantages afterward.

On the other hand, national authority still needs to take the stability and wealth of their citizens into consideration first. This keeps the equalization and impresses the respect with the contribution of their own people through the way using the national capital wisely.

To sum up, the government should give a hand to lift the poor up, this action reveals the mercy and sympathy to humanity. Besides, placing priority on their own country's benefits should be aware.

255 words

SAMPLE 31

Many people say the gap between rich and poor people is wider, as rich people become richer and poor people grow poorer.

What problems could this situation cause and what measures can be done to address those problems?

The economic inequality has been a common tendency in all corners of the world. This trend causes/results in numerous issues/problems and several solutions should be proposed to solve these problems.

There are two primary problems caused by the growing/increasing / huge gap between the rich and the poor. Firstly, inequality may increase social status differentiation creating more growing / increasing social distances. As a result, the poor feel disrespected so they have to fight for equality which leads to social insecurity. For example, the poor in the US organize wealth inequality protests in several states to ask for justice. Secondly, the rising tide of inequality stimulates social crime rate because the poor have to manage to survive. By way of illustration, the increasing number of burglaries or robbers has been witnessed as the simplest and fastest way to cover their cost of living and meet their basic demands.

Some simple measures should be implemented to deal with the problems caused by the widening gap between the poor and the rich. The governments should assist low-income earners in accessing training opportunities / the access of training opportunities that enable them to be fully developed/provide them with well-rounded development. As a consequence, they have equal chances to get the best employment prospects. In addition, the increase in average salary policy needs to be established to ensure employees could meet their basic needs. For instance, the average hourly wage in Ontario, Canada in 2017 increases to nearly 5.8 percentage from the previous year thanks to the rising living standard.

In conclusion, the problem of the rivalry between the poor and the rich can be tackled by effective measures on a governmental level.

279 words

SAMPLE 32

The computers are widely used in education and some people think that teachers should play an important role in the classroom. To what extent do you agree?

Nowadays, computers play an integral part in providing latest teaching method and upgrading quality of education. Nevertheless, it is in my opinion that teachers should play a major role in teaching their students.

To begin with, teachers are more flexible in the way of teaching students, because there are many kinds of students in classes. If a student falls behind his classmates, teachers need to tailor their teaching method to make him understand. The teachers have to explain the topic of lesson slowly and with a lot of repetition and elaboration. By doing so, students can understand improve their knowledge efficiently.

Also, having teachers to control classes will help students learn better. No one cannot imagine how a class would be if there is no teacher. For example, students from secondary school and high school are kind of naughty and easily distracted by things around them. Therefore, teachers have always to keep an eye on them and force them to pay attention to the lesson. Besides, teachers usually give homework assignments and challenge them by difficult tasks, and then students will be given high mark and compliment if they finish/ accomplish task perfectly. This is a great way for students to revise and recollect what they have been taught. By learning with teachers, students can receive many useful tips outside the lessons from their teachers, they also learn how to communicate with teachers and discuss problems with teachers well.

In conclusion, I am of the opinion that face to face traditional learning approach with teachers at school is the best way to acquire knowledge. By doing so, students help them to comprehend lessons easily.

274 words

SAMPLE 33

Some people think that all teenagers should be required to do unpaid work in their free time to help the local community. They believe this would be beneficial to both the individual teenager and society as a whole. Do you agree or disagree?

Society has received a lot of assistance from voluntary works of teenagers. Those unpaid works also bring about advantages to youngsters, however, I disagree that teenagers are all required to do that.

In the modern world, young generations are under high educational pressure so they should have free time for relaxation. They have to complete tons of home works as well as tests and exams in their class. Therefore, school is relatively similar to a full-time job, in which students are exploited by teachers, though the goal of this action is to expect students show their best ability. In addition, teenagers have the need of improving physical health, such as taking up sports and outdoor activities, which are recommended to be played regularly by the youth. Those physical exercises are extremely supportive of children's physical and mental health.

Moreover, voluntary work would be counter-productive if it is imposed as a compulsory one. As far as I am concerned, when my friends are forced to do specific things that they are not interested in, they may reduce their level of working performance or feel unwilling to do them. By contrast, youngsters would be more creative and devote more for what they have a passion for, even unpaid work. All over the world, an increasing number of teenagers are joining non-profit organizations such as NGOs, CDSD, or have a one-year exchange to do voluntary work in another developing country. After joining that, participants could receive certificates and, of course, improve their social skills.

In conclusion, I would agree that unpaid work should be done voluntarily instead of taking it as a compulsory one.

271 words

SAMPLE 34

Many people believe that international tourism is a bad thing for their country. What are the reasons? Solutions to change negative attitudes.

Nowadays, global tourism, a smokeless / non-smoke industry, has become a controversial issue with regard to its disadvantages. It is widely argued that worldwide travel may lead to a detrimental impact on host nations. From my perspective, this concern is not baseless and solutions must be applied to resolve the serious matters arising from international travel.

There are two main reasons why local people consider international tourism as a cause of drawbacks of some aspects in their country. The first one is degradation in local environment due to the lack of respect for holiday destinations of outbound tourists. Take renowned beaches in Vietnam as examples. The beaches such as Sam Son and Thuan An, have been seriously contaminated by visitors polluting and littering unconsciously. When visiting beauty spots, for individual benefits, many visitors would intend to exploit illegally ecological traits and thereby ruining the natural beauty of those sites. Another adverse influence might be social unrests such as sex trade and unfavorable inspiration to local young people. Indeed, they easily copy the provocative behaviour and inappropriate attire. Besides, the hidden threat coming from sexual demand may result in such social evils as human trafficking or sex crime.

To alleviate these negative problems, governments and international bodies are highly recommended to promulgate tougher laws against visitors breaking environmental rules. In my view, this solution should be combined with instructing foreign visitors how to keep the host nation's surroundings healthy. At the same time, tour guides should also urge visitors to reverence for the indigenous culture of their hosts. Also, bodies as the World Tourism Organization must enforce pertinent regulations on the tourism industry. First, they have to ensure that local operators are responsible for clearing litter in the ways that do not harm the environment. Secondly, banning red-light districts for foreigners as well as strengthening propaganda and awareness to combat prostitution.

In conclusion, only when the authorities are really heedful of the concerns of local residents may their view on international tourism be changed positively.

329 words

SAMPLE 35

Many students have to study subjects which they do not like. Some people think this is a complete waste of time. Do you agree or disagree with this statement?

Many people hold the belief that children should not be forced to acquire knowledge in fields they are not interested in. I completely disagree with this idea.

The advantage of being well-educated about many subjects is undeniable. The first reason is that information obtained during school life can be applicable in many aspects of their future life. Firstly, each subject has its own benefits/ perks. For examples, pupils can hate Physical Education but it helps them be stronger and healthier. Physics is a hard subject for many students but through it, they can know how to repair ruined electronic equipment or devices by themselves. Besides, learning many kinds of subjects allows students to have more opportunities to get a good job in the future. For instance, a person who is good at Economics and English has more chances to be applied than the one who only knows Economics.

Apart from the practical benefits expressed above, I believe that studying many subjects is not a waste of time if students have suitable/ appropriate learning methods. Because every subject has a connection to each other, it is much easier to link many subjects together rather than study one subject lonely. For example, in Physics, students learn many formulas and they can apply them in Meteorology to forecast the weather. The more subjects they study, the more knowledge in many fields they enhance.

In conclusion, I believe that spending time for the subjects students are not interested in is not time-wasting as some people think.

257 words

SAMPLE 36

Countries with long working days are more economically successful, but there are also some negative social consequences. To what extent do you agree or disagree?

The number of working hours per day has great impacts on employees. Although long working day results in the prosperity of some countries, it should not be encouraged because of several detrimental effects attached.

Firstly, it is undeniable that longer duration of work per day leads to lower productivity. In order to have efficiency at work, besides keeping attempts, people have to rest properly. Long working hours can possibly reduce the time of relaxation and other recreational activities, resulting in stress and pressure. If the situation endures, employees may lose their motivation at work and become discouraging, which surely reduce the level of job performance.

Next, if people have to work excessively, it can be counter-productive to the economic development will be at a stake. The reason for this statement is that a large amount of time put on work can reduce the time on entertainment and other services. There may be less consumption as well. The situation witnessed in Japan shows that as Japanese people are becoming honeybees at work, they do not engage in social activities much. Women in Japan do less shopping than those in the west, men have insufficient time to play sports or even hanging out, which leads to low consumption and decline in economic growth as consumption is an indispensable factor to boost the economy.

To sum up, working too long per day leads to severe consequences to individuals and the society as well. Governments should impose a law that regulates the minimum working hours for workers in order to remain productivity as well as the stable growth of the economy.

267 words

SAMPLE 37

Advertisements are getting their way into people's lives. Discuss the effects of advertisements on people. Should all ads be banned?

Give reasons for your answer and include any from your own knowledge or experience.

It is true that advertisement is gaining more and more popularity. While it is believed that this commercial activity is conducive to customers' convenience and companies' growth. Others argue that it can do nothing but a fraud and money wastage. In this essay, I will discuss both strength and weakness of this phenomenon.

It is true that some pieces of advertisement can awake customers' potential desire. Were it not for the televised images about the utility of iPhone, people hardly perceive handiness of this device from making phone calls to online chatting which they need to quicken their work. When it comes to cuisine, because of watching advertisements about fast food chains excessively, Vietnamese people might be aware of this dish and become addicted because of its convenience. Besides, these companies which pour money into advertisements/ commercial ads can generate profit as more customers are willing to purchase goods and services manufactured by these companies.

Yet the drawbacks of this can be foreseeable. For sake of profit, information about products can be distorted and overstated. Taking the case of a dietary supplement, in spite of limited efficiency for curing diseases, vivid advertisements can convey the messages that it is a panacea. Besides, it can stimulate people's desire over/ beyond their budget. For example, being frequently exposed to thousands of pop-up ads on websites about brand-name pieces of clothing can arouse in watchers the sense of belonging. Consequently, people are willing to spend an excessive amount of money on these luxurious items which turn out not to be essential to their life.

In a nutshell, providing that people are aware of dark sides of advertisement and the way that it can manipulate people's desire, this promotion activity is a workable channel to connect producers with potential consumers.

296 words

SAMPLE 38

Some people think that students in single-sex schools perform better academically. Others, however, believe that mixed schools provide children with better social skills for adult life. Discuss both these views and give your own opinion.

The question of whether enrolling in single-sex school or mixed is better for children development remains a source of controversy. While there are benefits to go to a single-sex school, there are also favorable reasons why it might be beneficial to select a diversified school.

On the one hand, there are a variety of reasons why studying in school with only boys or girls. Firstly, being taught in such schools will set the parents' mind at rest. Children will be well-educated and grown in a secure environment as none of the gender conflicts will ever occur. In addition, sex discrimination between two genders will never happen. Secondly, in the one-sided education system, learning direction will focus on subjects enhancing the profession of that gender. People will study about skills or knowledge for girls or boys only. For instance, girls will know how to cook or sew and even the rights of woman in the community. Therefore, pupils at such schools will strongly know not only girls' skills but also the understanding of subjects in relation to their sex.

On the other hand, the benefits of mixed school should also be taken into consideration. Firstly, students can access to information in many aspects of both genders without concentrating on any specified items. So the students can exchange the reality skills and support each other in future situations. And then one boy can even cook if he lives alone and similarly one girl can also undertake the hard and difficult works in charge by boys as usual. Secondly, studying in co-education system, school students have chances to show respect to the opposite sex as they grasp of the equality principle between men and women. So the traditional opinion putting emphasis on boys rather than girls will lose in society in the prospective years.

In conclusion, it seems evident that separate schools and joint schools have their own unique advantages for children education.

320 words

SAMPLE 39

In developing countries, children in rural communities have less access to education. Some people believe that the problem can be solved by providing more schools and teachers, while others think that the problem can be solved by providing computers and Internet access. Discuss both views and give your own opinion.

In many developing nations, children who live in remote areas do not have enough opportunities to pursue their studying. While some people argue that computers and Internet applications are the only ways to solve this problem, the opponents claim on the necessity of more schools and teachers. While there are certain benefits to provide an online method, I believe that students need to be involved in the social connection.

On the one hand, the suggestion to support computers and Internet access is useful in some ways. Firstly, rural communities tend to suffer from natural disasters. Therefore, studying at home through advanced technologies can be safer for students whose houses are in isolated regions. Secondly, children can make use of the time for traveling to school to help their parents to make ends meet because many of them are the main workforce in the family.

On the other hand, there are a variety of reasons why children need the presence of greater number of schools and teachers to make progress. Schooling is not only an environment to teach students academic knowledge but also orient young ones. Students should be educated fully in morality, physic, and social skills by interaction with teachers and other friends in the class. Moreover, teachers can give guidance and encourage students in specific situations whereas the computers connected to the Internet cannot. For instance, as children who are from a poor family can easily give up studying, teachers will give them useful advice to help them overcome difficulties in time.

In conclusion, both sides have their own advantages. Nevertheless, I do believe that schooling can create more positive influences on children who live in distant places.

279 words

SAMPLE 40

Some people think that the best way to reduce crime is to give longer prison sentences. Others, however, believe there are better alternative ways of reducing crime. Discuss both views and give your opinion?

In recent years, an increasing number of people are concerned about the effectiveness of longer prison sentences in reducing criminals. Some people believe that this strictly serious commitment can play an important role in preventing crime, while others state that there are also many ways to cope with this issue. I am strongly convinced by the latter view for the following reasons.

On the one hand, extending prison sentences causes several disadvantages to the country in terms of national budget. First, it is obvious that longer prison sentences can lead to a larger amount of national budget spent for prisoners, which is supposed to be spending for social welfare enhancement. This is mainly because of poverty, the root of crime committed. In many countries, both developing and developed ones, the truth has remained that crime is frequently connected to the crime. Therefore, in order to reduce crime from the root cause, the government should pay attention to boost the economic development, and then utilize most of the returns to improve social welfares, resulting in poverty reduction. For example, the government should make great efforts to provide residents reasonable education that brings them greater opportunities in the future. For that reason, it is essential for the government to enhance the social infrastructure to reduce the crime rate in the longer-term.

Moreover, focusing on strengthening authority system, especially national security is also a vital way of preventing criminals in short-term. For instance, equipping thousands of cutting-edge cameras in every corner of the street or increasing the existence of polices is not only an effective way to ensure the citizens' security but it also creates a better livable environment. If the government can quickly respond to the going-up crime rate by this way, it would be supported by most of the population in the country.

However, it is undeniable that longer prison sentences cannot play any role in reducing crime. There are, certainly, raising the public's awareness about the fact that criminal actions will be subject to more appropriate and severe punishment than before. Unfortunately, it is still difficult to solve the root of the dilemma in this way.

In conclusion, the most practical way to reduce crime in modern society is raising the people's living standard by guaranteeing them the easier access to better educational and healthy system. Meanwhile, longer prison sentences contribute to the increased awareness of the general public about criminal actions as individuals will have to face with extending years in prisons. This serves as a deterrent hindering people from committing crimes.

330 words

SAMPLE 41

Some people think that there should be some strict controls about noise. Others think that they could just make as much noise as they want. Discuss both views and give your opinion.

Some people hold the opinion that producing noise is one of their basic human rights, while others believed the level of noise should be strictly controlled. This essay will thoroughly discuss both of the views.

On the one hand, there are a variety of reasons why noise should be control under an acceptable level. Firstly, an excessive amount of noise would affect badly to people's health. A headache is a good example of some common symptoms that could happen to people who are exposed to high level of noise frequently, and this is even worse for senior citizens. In addition, people are more likely to have difficulties in concentrating on their work due to too much noise. For example, a student would not be able to focus on revising for his examination when his neighbors are having a party.

On the other hand, many people argue that they have the rights to make noise because it is one of many recreational activities. It is considered outrageous to make a person keep quiet during his favorite soccer match, or during a live concert. Furthermore, thanks to advances in technology, many sound-proof objects are made, such as windows, doors, and walls. Therefore, people are no longer required to keep silent and are able to produce noise to their likings.

In conclusion, there are some reasons why people should have the right to make noise. Nevertheless, I think the levels of noise should be limited so that it will not affect other individuals.

256 words

SAMPLE 42

Some people say that advertising encourages us to buy things that we really do not need. Others say that advertisements tell us about new products that may improve our lives?

It is the fact that advertisement has long been a topic of great concern nowadays. While I agree that advertising aims to persuade people to buy unnecessary things, I still hold the belief that it also brings numerous advantages which may help to improve our lives.

On the one hand, it is undeniable that advertising gives the customers more options to buy things which is most suitable for them. In other words, advertisement informs us about/in terms of/regarding different new products or services. Therefore, buyers can know and understand exactly about the products' features, which help them to come to accurate decisions. On a larger scale, advertisement leads to prices wars between different brands on the market, which will slash the prices of the products as well as improve their qualities. As a result, the buyers will receive huge benefits from the prices to the qualities due to the appearance of advertisement.

On the other hand, advertising is possible to make the customers spend money on things which they do not need actually/in real-life. That is because advertisements usually magnify/exaggerate the real value of the products and make people feel that they really need these products. Therefore, the purchasers are easily swayed by advertising and then they may buy these things although they might not be useful or have good qualities. For example, in 2015, a survey from Youth Newspaper showed that over 70 percent of customers were not satisfied with the qualities of the products which they knew through advertising.

In conclusion, although advertisements may have some drawbacks about telling inaccurate information about the products, which encourages us to overspend for unnecessary things, it cannot be denied that our lives cannot be improved without advertisements, especially in the free market economies. If we can solve these problems, advertising could be the perfect tool for both customers and producers.

309 words

SAMPLE 43

Many people hold the belief that only high-flyers should be given priority to pursue tertiary education rather than having wide access to a majority of young people. In my opinion, enrolling in university education is the basic human right and this should not be restricted.

There are a variety of reasons why all people should be allowed to attend university and one of which is that a college education prepares most young people to meet high – level qualifications. Indeed, employers are seeking for recruiting employees with at least one degree in a competitive working environment today. Doubtlessly, university graduates with fundamentally theoretical knowledge can quickly adapt to their jobs and contributes to nations' prosperity.

Furthermore, I strongly believe that broadening opportunities to enter universities reduces the shortage of brainworker resources. According to recent reports in the New York Times newspapers, the sufficiency of brain-workers has positive effects such as the expansion of potential enterprises, the development of working environment and the increase of industrial innovations. As a result, many nations can accelerate these beneficial impacts thanks to the efficient provision of the graduate labor force.

It is argued that only the very best academic students with high marks can obtain an academic qualification. However, having good marks does not guarantee whether students are intelligent or not because they usually study studiously. Obviously, curricula in universities are different from those in lower education because learners can deal with many practical projects. Therefore, students with poor academic performances can expand their mind and success if they learn in their desirable majors in universities.

To conclude, I totally agree that university education should be available to a large proportion of people because university education plays an integral part in providing students with essential knowledge and skills to embark on a career later in life. The university qualifications and knowledge enable students to achieve their goals.

267 words

SAMPLE 44

Some people think that in the modern world we are more dependent on each other, while others think that people have become more independent. Discuss both views and give your own opinion.

The question whether we are becoming increasingly dependent or independent on each other in today's society remains a source of controversy. In my opinion, people in modern life will be more independent than in the past.

The reasons why we are over-reliant on other people vary. Firstly, some activities always demand/ require cooperation between the partners to survive and develop, and the interaction is a key element of existence. For instance, we need both sellers and buyers in business, students and teachers in education and patients need care from doctors. Secondly, life is more complex and difficult because the cost of living has increased. The young person tends to rely on their parent for a long time. In particular, when they need to buy a house, they require their parents to support them a lot of money.

However, I am of the opinion that people are gaining more independence. The developing of technology lead people to work separately. Workers will work with robots and machines rather than working with others and students tend to take part in online courses instead of going to universities. Furthermore, people have to live away from family for working and studying. People live in rural area move to a big city such as Hanoi city where many big universities and big companies are based. These migrant employees will have a private life, hence they earn money for living without supporting from family.

In conclusion, while some clear arguments prove that people have to depend on each other, I strongly believe that life will be highly independent.

262 words

SAMPLE 45

Some people think that a sense of competition in children should be encouraged. Others believe that children who are taught to co-operate rather than compete become more useful adults.

Discuss both these views and give your own opinion.

While some people hold the opinion that students' competitive spirit should be enhanced to achieve success; the opponents of this idea argue that co-operation is more useful. Although I agree that competition is important, I believe that co-operating ability/ cooperation skills are the key children's future success.

On the one hand, living in a competitive environment brings various benefits to students. Firstly, the spirit of competition creates motivation for studying. Unlike adults, children rarely show their interest for in studying. There more, this healthy rivalry ought to be utilized to engage students and improve their participation/ involvement level. Secondly, competition is a natural yet effective way to enhance student's individual work due to the fact that every young learner will make great effort to become winners.

On the other hand, it seems to me that co-operation is a better skill to be fostered. Whereas competition encourages individual work, co-operation allows students to develop their ability to work in teams, which is an important skill that most employers are seeking today. To be specific, most employers nowadays are looking for candidates who can work productively in groups, not individually. Thus, co-operation prepares students more chances of success for future job interviews. In addition, co-operating gives students opportunities to learn from their peers and support others to achieve certain goals instead of defeating each other. This spirit helps nurture fair play and truly talented adults, not those who take advantage of using bad tricks to acquire their aims.

In conclusion, while it is impossible to deny the benefits of competition in education, I think that teaching co-operation skill in schools results in better residents for our society.

275 words

SAMPLE 46

It is generally agreed that society benefits from the work of its members. Compare the contribution. Which type of contribution do you think is more valued by your society? Give specific reasons to support your answer.

It is true that artists and scientists make a huge contribution to our lives and play a crucial role in formation and development of our society. All of these achievements deserve respect from the public; however, I suppose that scientists' contribution is highly recognized and more appreciated than that of artists.

On the one hand, works in art improve people's moral and spiritual values. For instance, singers and musicians reduce the boredom of our lives and mix many colors into the moral life through their music. In addition, thanks to meaningful rhythm and lyrics, people feel entertained, gain knowledge and learn about the culture, history of our countries and other nations thanks to artists' brilliant performances. Artists' masterpieces not only help people realize who we are, but also educate and enhance our morality.

On the other hand, achievements in scientific fields play an integral part in our material lives. An obvious example of this is that many advances in technology such as cars, computers and household appliances shorten people's distance and decrease workload/ improve the productivity. Thanks to scientific researches, many serious diseases are cured completely; therefore, human health is increasingly improved. Scientists also provide us with many precious theories in mathematics, science, and chemistry.

No matter how considerable artists' contribution is, I believe that society tends to appreciate scientists more. Scientists are usually entitled to be intelligent experts with higher salaries, prestige, and reputation. Although some artists are wealthier and have more influences than famous scientists, these cases are negligible. In general, scientists are higher evaluated and even more respected by society.

To summarize, the contribution of artists and scientists are both essential to our society in terms of spiritual and material fields. It is my belief that artists should achieve the high appreciation if they fulfill their tasks successfully.

301 words

SAMPLE 47

The world natural resources are being consumed at an ever-increased rate.

What are the dangers of this situation? What should we do?

In recent years, the world is facing the problem of overconsumption of natural resources. This leads to a number of serious consequences which should be tackled promptly.

This overexploitation of environmental resources has damaging impacts not only on the living habitat but also on the community as a whole. In terms of living environment, contamination of land, water, and air has increased to an alarming level due to too much reliance on natural energy resources. For example, coal is the main power energy in China and Australia. The burning of coal and oil results in air pollution and global warming, through the emissions of greenhouse gases. In terms of society, deforestation destroys large areas of tropical rainforests and overfishing devastates fish stock. As a result, farmers have to fight the flash floods due to the forest degradation and a majority of fishing villages are predicted to disappear in next decades.

Therefore, some urgent measures should be taken by the government to solve such issues. Firstly, citizens should be encouraged to switch to alternative energy resources. In particular, governments need to largely invest in green energy like solar and wind energy to make them feasible to the society. Secondly, local and international authorities should strictly impose and enforce environmental laws and regulations to protect and conserve those invaluable natural resources. As a result, natural resources can be exploited effectively and those who deliberately break the law will be severely punished.

In conclusion, the over-consumption of natural resources has detrimental effects not only on the environment but also the society. Therefore, several actions should be implemented to tackle this terrible situation such as transferring to alternative sources of energy and reinforcing environmental laws.

282 words

SAMPLE 48

Some countries build specialized sports facilities for top athletes to train instead of providing sports facilities that everyone can use. Is this a positive or negative development?

In some nations, sports infrastructure for professional athletes recently has been invested greatly; meanwhile, it seems that sports areas for citizens use have been ignored. Although the investment in public sports facilities could be a suggested idea for the national sports training improvement, I believe that it might not be the optimal decision in general.

In my opinion, devoting a huge amount of money to specialized sports facilities perhaps would bring about some supreme international achievements for the country. Obviously, when there is sufficient provision/offer of the best-qualified training conditions, sport-players would attain important prizes far more easily. Particularly, in the international tournaments or Olympic, they might be able to compete with other athletes from a great number of nations and get gold, silver or bronze medals. In other words, applying the eligible devices for a professional sportsman is to give them more chances to win prizes and to raise the national status in the global sports competitions.

However, I think that small budget allocation on public sports facilities is not a compelling decision due to the fact that sports areas for amateurs are also important. Firstly, by providing training places such as city swimming pools, tennis courts or football fields where everyone can access easily, widespread provision of sports facility in public places would definitely boost people' motivation/incentive to take part in their favorite sports, leading to the awareness of health and keeping in shape in the community. Secondly, if these places were opened to all people, there would be a plenty of chances for trainers to find out potential talents from these local sports centres and train them to be sports stars in the future. This is truly a good way for overall sports developments.

In conclusion, I believe that building places for top sportsmen is a positive way to promote the records of athletes in the international competitions, but the local training places should be also invested for the physical conditions of people in society.

328 words

SAMPLE 49

Some people think that people who choose a job early and keep doing it are more likely to get a satisfying career life than those who frequently change jobs.

To what extent do you agree or disagree?

The question whether working a permanent job or changing job frequently is beneficial for employees still remains a source of controversy. While there are lots of advantages to jumping to another job, I do believe that staying in the same work would make people achieve a successful career.

There are several reasons why I would argue that changing job frequently has/ brings more disadvantages rather than advantages. On the one hand, although embarking on a new career may offer people higher salary, or higher position which are usually main reasons for them to make a decision of switching, they also need to restart everything in the beginning such as engaging/ bending new company culture, building new relationship with new colleagues that take them a lot of time to build instead of focusing on the main job's target. Furthermore, if workers change their job from their ex-company to a competitor, they may damage their image which they have built for a long time, thus, they might get a low reputation from customers.

On the other hand, sticking in the same organization would lead people to a stable career life. Firstly, it is much easier for these people to have good job prospects and build a strong relationship with colleagues when they work in one company for a long time. For example, as a Sale Manager, with my 10 years experience in the same company, I can easily to get a deal from my customer without taking too much time. Secondly, as a seniority employee, people can have benefits to get support easily from their boss or their colleagues when they need so that they might have more comfortable during their working life, thus, they can have more time for themselves or their own family.

In conclusion, changing job may provide employees some benefits, I would argue that remaining in the same company would be more positive.

315 words

SAMPLE 50

Discuss the topic: Should scientists conduct scientific research on mummies?

The fact that whether scientists should do a dissection on mummies or not remains a source of controversy. While I accept that many people come up with the idea that we should not conduct these kinds of research, I believe that analyzing mummies brings about a wide range of knowledge which is beneficial for our life.

On the one hand, this action is unethical to some extent and we need to let these dead people rest in peace. This is because when discovering a tomb, scientists may have to dismantle a lot of things, not just only the tomb but also traps, material accompanied with it. Moreover, it is prohibitively expensive to fully understand about the ancients. In the time when the earth is promptly warming, the poor are struggling with the scarcity of food, taking a research on dead bodies is not needful.

On the other hand, there are various reasons why mummies should be discovered. If national revenue is allocated to conduct further studies of mummies, the prehistoric world would be much more explicit and people would acquire a deep insight of human evolution. Ancient mummies/ dead bodies can provide a great source of information about the health of early civilizations, which may help us better treat diseases today. Moreover, mummies could be absolute damaged as time goes by. Only by being investigated, they are conserved at the best of times and places.

In conclusion, what can be learned from studying human remains is important for history and science so as long as having enough/ sufficient facilities, scientists should prudently conduct research on mummies.

266 words

SAMPLE 51

The government should spend money on railways rather than roads. To what extent do you agree or disagree?

It is believed that the national budget should be allocated to railway systems instead of roads. However, I disagree with this statement due to the indispensable role of this travelling infrastructure.

In my point of view, train journeys may entail some potential risks which can be the deterrents to investing in this system. Specifically, many accidents on railways are due to the damages caused by unexpected disasters on trains and lines. In this case, people cannot guarantee their own safety since natural phenomena are unavoidable. Besides, railway systems can hardly meet the diverse needs of customers. In fact, the train is the only suitable vehicle for railways; however, it is more often used for travelling long distances with few stops. Moreover/In addition, travelling by train means lack of space and privacy. Therefore, investment in the railway system may be a waste as people cannot take advantages of this mean of transportation.

On the other hand, roads should receive greater attention as it is worth the budget. First, the expansion and modernization of roads can improve the appearance of cities. Specifically, wider roads eliminate the problem of crowded and unorganized streets; therefore, they will look more modern and beautiful. Secondly, developing road system allows people to drive their own vehicle, which is convenient in all aspects. For example, while the safety of passengers can be under their own control, they still have to freedom to change the destination or do whatever they want. Finally, road expansion results in the use of a wider range of transportation means such as buses, cars and so on. This variation can suit the requirements of different people; for example, some can bicycle to exercise while going to work.

In conclusion, I believe the government should prioritize road systems over railways because of its efficiency, convenience, and safety.

302 words

SAMPLE 52

Young people are important resources to their country, but governments may ignore some problems faced by young people in running the country. Please show those problems and give your ideal suggestions to solve them.

Recently, the issue of juvenile crime has been in the limelight and has given rise to a heated/ enthusiastic debate in the public. As the saying goes, "There is no smoke without fire", the government is blamed for not paying enough attention to the young's problems. Since they are important resources to the country, they deserve better care.

Firstly, the particular problem challenging young people is unemployment. It is believed that this situation is caused mainly by bad governance and poor education system. Most are not well prepared for the job market as skills have not been imparted to them during schooling. Since the government is responsible for the lack of jobs, it's high time they did something to deal with this dilemma. Top priority must be given to education. The young should be provided with the best education at the time and infrastructure should be improved to surround them with the best condition. Moreover, the government should create more employment opportunities as well as launch a campaign to ensure young people's voices are heard in the debate around the future goals.

Secondly, the family problem is another big issue faced by the youth. A complex family background makes them angry, anxious and depressed all the time. These feelings can affect other areas of their lives such as school and friendships. Hence, the best way to deal with this issue is reducing family conflicts. Local governments should take charge of reconciling conflicts if there are any. In case the family breaks up, adolescents should be given psychological support to get over this hard time and get back to the daily life.

In conclusion, young people are facing many problems nowadays. The government should take it seriously and act out to protect them. Since the young are important resources to the country, they should be physically and mentally helped in any possible situations.

312 words

CONCLUSION

Thank you again for downloading this book on *"IELTS Writing Task 2 Samples: Over 50 High-Quality Model Essays for Your Reference to Gain a High Band Score 8.0+ In 1 Week (Book 12)."* and reading all the way to the end. I'm extremely grateful.

If you know of anyone else who may benefit from the useful task 2 writing sample essays for their reference, please help me inform them of this book. I would greatly appreciate it.

Finally, if you enjoyed this book and feel that it has added value to your work and study in any way, please take a couple of minutes to share your thoughts and post a REVIEW on Amazon. Your feedback will help me to continue to write other books of IELTS topic that helps you get the best results. Furthermore, if you write a simple REVIEW with positive words for this book on Amazon, you can help hundreds or perhaps thousands of other readers who may want to improve their English writing skills sounding like a native speaker. Like you, they worked hard for every penny they spend on books. With the information and recommendation you provide, they would be more likely to take action right away. We really look forward to reading your review.

Thanks again for your support and good luck!

If you enjoy my book, please write a POSITIVE REVIEW on Amazon.

-- Rachel Mitchell --

CHECK OUT OTHER BOOKS

Go here to check out other related books that might interest you:

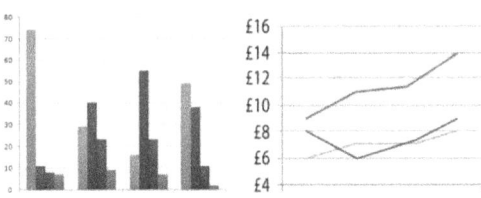

Ielts Academic Writing Task 1 Samples : Over 35 High Quality Samples for Your Reference to Gain a High Band Score 8.0+ In 1 Week (Book 1)

https://www.amazon.com/dp/B076V62DZC

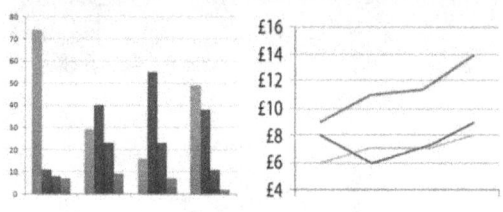

Ielts Academic Writing Task 1 Samples : Over 35 High Quality Samples for Your Reference to Gain a High Band Score 8.0+ In 1 Week (Book 2)

https://www.amazon.com/dp/B076VDY58V

Shortcut To English Collocations: Master 2000+ English Collocations In Used Explained Under 20 Minutes A Day (5 books in 1 Box set)

https://www.amazon.com/dp/B06W2P6S22

IELTS Writing Task 1 + 2: The Ultimate Guide with Practice to Get a Target Band Score of 8.0+ In 10 Minutes a Day

https://www.amazon.com/dp/B075DFYPG6

IELTS Speaking Strategies: The Ultimate Guide With Tips, Tricks, And Practice On How To Get A Target Band Score Of 8.0+ In 10 Minutes A Day.

https://www.amazon.com/dp/B075JCW65G

Shortcut To Ielts Writing: The Ultimate Guide To Immediately Increase Your Ielts Writing Scores.

https://www.amazon.com/dp/B01JV7EQGG

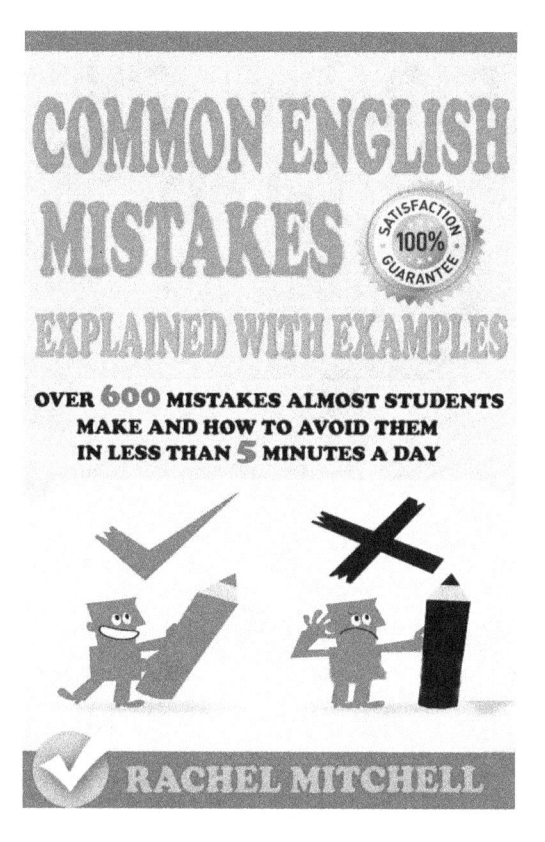

Common English Mistakes Explained With Examples: Over 600 Mistakes Almost Students Make and How to Avoid Them in Less Than 5 Minutes A Day

https://www.amazon.com/dp/B072PXVHNZ

Paraphrasing Strategies: 10 Simple Techniques For Effective Paraphrasing In 5 Minutes Or Less

https://www.amazon.com/dp/B071DFG27Q

Legal Vocabulary In Use: Master 600+ Essential Legal Terms And Phrases Explained In 10 Minutes A Day

http://www.amazon.com/dp/B01L0FKXPU

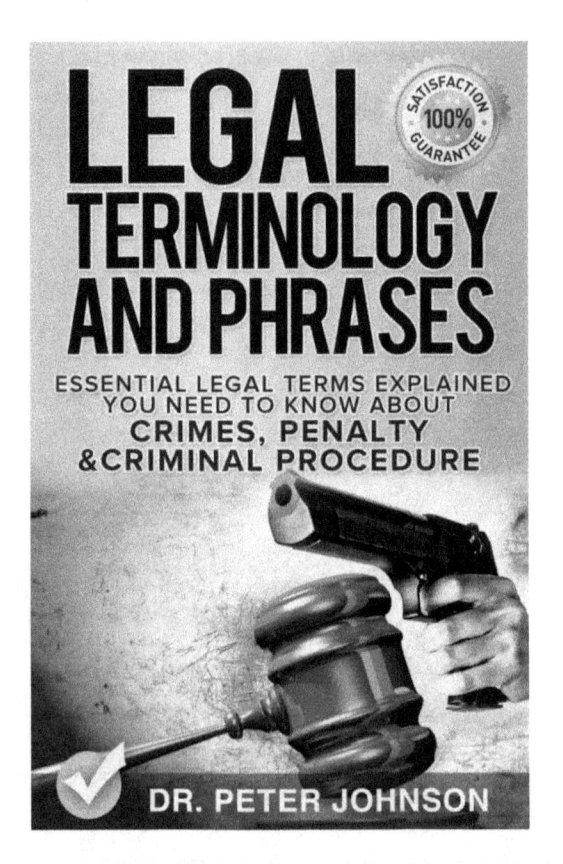

Legal Terminology And Phrases: Essential Legal Terms Explained You Need To Know About Crimes, Penalty And Criminal Procedure

http://www.amazon.com/dp/B01L5EB54Y

Productivity Secrets For Students: The Ultimate Guide To Improve Your Mental Concentration, Kill Procrastination, Boost Memory And Maximize Productivity In Study

http://www.amazon.com/dp/B01JS52UT6

Daughter of Strife: 7 Techniques On How To Win Back Your Stubborn Teenage Daughter

https://www.amazon.com/dp/B01HS5E3V6

Parenting Teens With Love And Logic: A Survival Guide To Overcoming The Barriers Of Adolescence About Dating, Sex And Substance Abuse

https://www.amazon.com/dp/B01JQUTNPM

UNDERSTANDING MEN IN RELATIONSHIPS

THE TOP 44 IRRESISTIBLE QUALITIES MEN WANT IN A WOMAN

SATISFACTION 100% GUARANTEE

KELVIN KING

http://www.amazon.com/dp/B01K0ARNA4

www.ingramcontent.com/pod-product-compliance
Lightning Source LLC
LaVergne TN
LVHW040640250225
804422LV00004B/602